the anima

Herbal Recipe Book

herbal goodies for horses and other animals

notes & recipes

by Dr. Christine King

Published by Dr. Christine King

Anima Books

Issaquah, WA 98027

animavet.com

ISBN: 0-9674926-2-9
ISBN-13: 978-0-9674926-2-9

Please Note

The U.S. Food & Drug Administration and Department of Agriculture prohibit claims of nutritional or medicinal benefit for substances they do not regard as "food" or have not approved as "medicine." For this reason, information about the herbal blends described in this book is limited to their contents, suggested use, and what Dr. King intended when formulating them. Please view all statements about individual herbs and the herbal blends as simply one veterinarian's considered opinion.

This book is not intended to be a substitute for veterinary care. Please partner with a veterinarian to ensure the very best care for your animal

Contents

Why Feed Herbs?

Using herbs in horses is a no-brainer for me. Horses are herbivores; they are designed by nature to live on a diet of plants. Although horses and other herbivores do occasionally eat animal-source items, generally they do so by choice only in situations of nutritional deficiency, when their needs are not being met by their vegetarian diet. (While a horse may eat a baloney sandwich, that doesn't mean the baloney was the draw, or even that it was liked.) When an adequate quantity, quality, and variety of plant material is available, horses choose—and thrive on—plants.

So, plants are the principal nutrient source for horses. The neat thing is that many plants also have medicinal properties. Not only do we humans know that, animals seem to instinctively know it, too. (In fact, we may have learned much of it from them.) Self-medication is a specific behavior that biologists have only lately begun to study but that indigenous people and herdsmen have known about for as long as humans and animals have been living together. Both wild and domesticated animals have been observed to select specific plants and even eat soil, clay, and charcoal when ill, injured, parasitized, or otherwise unhealthy. I have witnessed this behavior many times in my patients. In fact, I rely on it when I'm unsure of what to provide an animal for nutritional or medicinal benefit.

Herbs as food and medicine

Taking a metaphorical leaf from nature's book, in my veterinary practice I use herbs for two primary purposes: as food and as medicine. Of course, there's a great deal of overlap there, because it's as Hippocrates advised:

> *"Let thy food be thy medicine, and thy medicine thy food."*

In fact, I suspect that one of the ways medicinal herbs aid in healing is by providing nutrients which have been lacking in the animal's diet. Certainly, there's more going on biochemically (and, I believe, energetically) with the more potent medicinal herbs. But for me the line is very much blurred between nutrition and medicine.

Still, to keep it as simple as possible, I've divided the recipes in this book into two general categories:

❀ herbs as food (chapter 2)

❀ herbs as medicine (chapter 3)

You may be tempted to jump straight to the second group of recipes, especially if your horse has a current medical problem. But please give the first group of recipes a good look, too. When we eat well, there is less need for medicine of any kind, whether herbal, homeopathic, nutritional, or pharmaceutical.

Although I use each of those classes of medicine in my veterinary practice, time and again I've found that simply changing the horse's diet can be enough to correct whatever medical, performance, or even behavioral problem I was called out to treat. Whether horse or human, our bodies are designed to be self-maintaining and self-repairing, and that's the way they function—provided that they have all the nutrients they need to do so.

By the way, this book is primarily about herbs for horses, but I do use herbs in other herbivores and in dogs and cats as well, both nutritionally and medicinally. Where appropriate, you'll see notes on suggested use of the blend for dogs and cats.

More on herbs as food

Here's my philosophy on feeding horses: Regardless of age, breed, occupation, dollar value, performance level, or health status, horses do best when fed a diet that is as close as possible to what nature has provided for them—a wide variety of plants that changes with the seasons.

"As close as possible" will mean different things for different horses and in different circumstances, but the fundamentals are the same for all. While the typical performance horse is required to do far more than his wild or feral counterparts, his physiology is the same. He is still a horse, and he will do best when fed a diet to which the horse's digestive system and metabolism have adapted over the millennia.

the horse's natural diet

The horse's natural diet consists of many different grasses, legumes, and various other meadow and woodland plants. Naturalists estimate that wild or feral horses may browse from at least 50 different types of plants, depending on what's available in that location at that time. The variety comes not just from the range of plant species available, but also from the variations in plant types, parts (roots, stems, bark, leaves, flowers, fruit, seeds), and constituents with the different seasons.

One might argue that wild or feral horses eat this way because they must, simply to survive. There certainly is a "make do" element to the way wild or feral horses live in most parts of the world. But having practiced both conventionally and holistically during my veterinary career, I can attest to the health benefits gained by attempting to replicate that variety in the way we feed domesticated horses.

the typical domestic horse's diet

In growing energy-rich foods for our horses and other livestock, we have sacrificed variety for calories, convenience, and economy. The typical domestic horse's diet is very limited in variety, particularly if the horse has little or no access to natural pastures, woodlands, or other uncultivated areas.

Most horses are fed just one or two types of hay, day in and day out. While there may be a few other plants mixed in, most hays are grown as monocrops—an entire field sown with just one species of grass or legume. That's not the way nature does it; and it's not the best way of maintaining healthy soils, healthy plants, and healthy animals. *Diversity* is a fundamental property of a healthy ecosystem, and of a healthy diet.

Even if the horse does have access to pasture, many pastures are overgrazed, seeded with just a few human-selected plant species, or treated with herbicides, so they provide little variety or range of plant nutrients. Regardless of whether some alfalfa or a grain-based concentrate is added, the typical equine diet is profoundly lacking in variety when compared with the horse's natural diet.

Not only is variety of plant species lacking in this diet, so too is the quality and quantity of phytonutrients (plant-source nutrients), because processing and storage cause a progressive decline in the more fragile phytonutrients, including vitamins, essential fatty acids, and various other antioxidant substances naturally found in abundance in fresh plant material.

Most processed horse feeds are "fortified" with vitamins and minerals, and some these days even contain added antioxidants. But in my opinion the quality, variety, complexity, and *synergy* of phytonutrients cannot be completely replicated or replaced with factory-made supplements, especially those that contain man-made or industrialized ingredients. For all our knowledge and ingenuity, we still cannot recompose an apple out of a collection of its analyzed parts.

Obviously, horses can survive on the limited variety provided by the typical diet, but they do not *thrive* on this diet. Over time, various chronic health problems appear that we take for granted are simply caused by "aging." The truth is that these conditions are largely preventable with good management, which includes good nutrition. The same can be said for many other common ailments, such as colic, heaves, laminitis, and exercise-related muscle disorders. Good food is fundamental to good health, and good food for a horse includes a wide variety of suitable plants.

providing more variety

To recap, horses are designed to get all of their nutrient needs from plants and the soils in which they grow. But the twin keys here are quality and variety. Healthy soils are soils that are rich—in both numbers and diversity—in microbes, minerals, and organic matter. Healthy soils make for healthy plants, which make for healthy horses.

The vitamins and minerals found in plants generally are more bioavailable (more readily absorbed and put to use by the body) than those added to the diet in an inorganic, chelated, or otherwise isolated or artificial form. The plant has already done the work of assimilating minerals from the soil, enmeshing them with its own living molecules, and thus putting them to use in its own biochemical processes.

Nature has already figured this out for the horse. We would be wise to follow her lead and feed a diet that consists of a wide variety of plants and plant parts that have had little or no processing—i.e. whole foods. The recipes in this book consist, for the most part, of whole-food,* plant-based nutrition.

(*Even though almost all of the herbs used in these recipes comprise only certain parts of a plant [e.g. just the root or the fruit] and some are powdered, they are still considered "whole foods" because they are not processed beyond being cut and dried, and in some cases powdered. They are not extracts or isolates, nor in any other way reduced or refined; they are still essentially in their natural state.)

The more variety we offer of plants grown in well-tended soils, the more likely the body will get all it needs in the way of primary nutrients (carbohydrates, fats, proteins, vitamins, minerals) and cofactors (trace minerals, enzymes, antioxidants, beneficial bacteria, and probably some other substances we don't yet know about). And the less we'll need to use supplements—including the ones in this book—to meet the shortfall and keep our horses healthy for life. *All* of these nutrients are essential for maintaining good health, tissue repair, vitality, and longevity.

Ideally, the horse would get the bulk of his nutrient needs by grazing healthy pastures, meadows, and woodland areas, with any shortfall made up by feeding a mix of good quality hays (grasses and legumes) and perhaps more calorie-dense supplements as needed. But when good grazing is not available or advisable for whatever reason, I use herbs to add variety and fill in the nutritional gaps that are inevitable with a hay-based or highly processed diet. The recipes in the next chapter (HERBS AS FOOD) are formulated to do just that.

While on the subject of variety, I try to source hays and herbs from as many different geographic areas as I can. The less fossil fuels burned in getting the plants from soil to horse, the better. On the other hand, gathering plants from several different areas ensures that local or regional soil deficiencies or defective farming practices have less of an impact on the overall diet. Another consideration is whether to support local agriculture exclusively or also support small farmers in other parts of the globe. These are issues you must explore and decide for yourself.

The herbs used in these recipes

There are a mind-boggling number and variety of plants that have nutritional or medicinal properties. On every continent except Antarctica, there exists the plant life necessary to support the life and health of the animals who live there. (And one might argue that in Antarctic waters the role is filled by algae and other tiny phyto-organisms.) One way to put it is that there is tremendous "redundancy" built into the system. Lots of substitutions and variations on the theme are possible here, thanks to the creativity and generosity of nature.

When developing these herbal goodies for horses, I decided to stick with plants that are native or naturalized to North America, because this is where I currently live and practice. If you are more at home with the plants of Europe, Africa, South America, Asia, or Australia, then please substitute as you like.

safety

I also took care to choose herbs that are known to be safe for horses to eat in fairly liberal quantities. The herbs used in these recipes have a long history of nutritional or medicinal use in horses. That was very important to me, as not all medicinal herbs are safe to use in horses or have a wide safety margin in this species. All of the herbs used in these recipes have a wide safety margin in horses, except where noted.

palatability

Particularly when formulating the primarily nutritive blends, I chose herbs that are readily eaten by horses. Just as we do, horses select their foods in large part by taste and smell. I took that into account when formulating these blends, so the results are both nutritious and delicious. (I know that because I sometimes make a tea of the seasonal *Meadow Blends,* and I often take one of the *Vitality* blends in a glass of water.) The most important thing when I'm formulating is that the blend must do what I intend for it to do nutritionally or medicinally. A close second, though, is that it must taste good, or at least be tolerable.

Even so, taste can be a highly individual thing, and our appetites for specific foods can change according to our body's needs. That is the basis of the self-medication behavior observed in horses and other animals (and also in humans). Having seen this behavior many times in my practice (and experienced it first-hand when grocery shopping), I have no trouble believing this phenomenon to be real and relevant to the horse's health and well-being.

So, the best approach when feeding herbs to horses may be to offer a variety of well-chosen herbs individually and free choice, and let the horse choose what, when, and how much to eat. The problem is that this approach is not practical for most people. I continue to explore this issue of free-choice herbs, but in the meantime the blends included in this book do a fairly good job of being acceptable to, and meeting the needs of, most horses in most circumstances.

❀❀

Herbs as Food

Leafy Blends

All of the recipes in this chapter are designed primarily for nutritional benefit. The first five recipes are leafy blends of whole or cut leaves, stems, roots, flowers, berries, and seeds that are formulated primarily for horses and other grazing animals. They contribute to the horse's diet by providing:

❀ a wider variety of plant species and plant parts

❀ a source of supplemental nutrients that is all-natural, plant-based, and minimally processed (i.e. mostly whole foods, and mostly raw)

❀ a blend of herbs that is designed to support all of the organ systems commonly under stress in domesticated horses

❀ seasonal variation

The two "flagship" recipes are the seasonal blends of meadow and woodland plants called the *Spring-Summer* and *Autumn-Winter Meadow Blends*. The "special needs" blends that follow (*Competition, Cornucopia,* and *Mobility)* are variations on this theme. These five blends are especially useful for horses with limited access to healthy grazing and foraging.

As I discuss in chapter 1, my preference is for horses to be allowed access to a wide variety of fresh plant material every day, according to what is available and advisable for the individual. (More on advisability in a moment.) There is an indefinable yet unmistakable *vitality* to fresh, living plant material that is lost in the cutting and drying process. No matter how good the dried herbs are, and how well formulated or appropriate the blend, they are not a patch on what is growing fresh and in season.

Under certain circumstances, such as with obesity, a history of pasture-associated laminitis or colic, and developmental orthopedic disorders, it is wise to restrict grazing when plant sugars and starches are likely to be high. That is a topic for another day, and a call you should make in consultation with your veterinarian.

It is these horses who most need, and most benefit from, supplemental feeding with a variety of herbs. Fresh is best, but when that's not possible, a well-chosen blend of dried herbs can save the day.

When buying herbs, choose organically grown herbs whenever possible. Not only is it the healthiest option for your horse, it is the healthiest thing for the soil and the entire ecosystem. So, please follow the mantra: *"organic if possible."*

Powdered Blends

The final three recipes in this chapter are all variations on the central theme of helping to meet the animal's micronutrient needs with all-natural and mostly whole-food sources:

❀ plants

❀ chlorophyll-rich algae

❀ sea vegetables*

❀ naturally occurring clays and salts that contain a wide range of trace minerals

(* I use sea vegetables or seaweeds very little in domestic animals, preferring to use mostly terrestrial sources of nutrients for terrestrial animals. In this, as in all things, I'm trying to follow nature's lead.)

All three blends in this section use powdered or finely flaked ingredients. The first two blends are formulated primarily for horses, and the last is formulated for dogs.

Although this chapter is titled HERBS AS FOOD, it is important to note that these blends are not formulated according to the National Research Council (NRC) guidelines for nutritional supplements in horses or dogs. They are designed simply to "fill in the gaps" that are theoretical yet anticipated in a basic diet which so often is limited in variety and freshness.

When a particular nutrient is known or expected to be lacking, such as calcium in home-made diets for dogs and selenium in forages grown in the Pacific northwest, then that nutrient should be provided in NRC-recommended amounts—ideally using a species-appropriate and natural form of that nutrient (e.g. bone for calcium in dogs, and a legume such as alfalfa for calcium in horses).

I cannot emphasize enough that when the basic diet provides a wide variety of fresh, wholesome, species-appropriate foods, then there is little need for supplements of any kind. For example, I do not feed my dog *Vitality canid* every day. Instead, she gets a wide variety of fresh foods (including bones) as her basic diet. Likewise, horses can be only sparingly supplemented when the basic diet is good.

Each recipe is given its own two-page spread so that you can set the book out flat and make notes as you go. Feel free to experiment, make adjustments and substitutions according to your horse's preferences—and whenever and however you can in your particular situation, try offering the individual herbs free-choice.

Spring-Summer Meadow Blend

This seasonal blend is formulated to provide some of the meadow and woodland plants available to horses during the warmer months of the year. It is designed to expand the variety of plant-source nutrients in the horse's diet, using plants or plant parts that are naturally available during the growing season.

Ingredients:

herbs	proportions	to make 3 lbs	other amount or substitution
cleavers	1	4 oz.	
dandelion leaf	1	4 oz.	
dandelion root	1	4 oz.	
elder berries	1	4 oz.	
hawthorn leaf & flower	1	4 oz.	
marshmallow root	2	8 oz.	
nettle leaf	2	8 oz.	
raspberry leaf	1	4 oz.	
red clover leaf & flower	1	4 oz.	
rose hips	1	4 oz.	

Instructions:

Measure out all herbs and mix together well. (Note: dried raspberry leaf tends to clump, so break up any clumps as you mix.) Store the blend in a dry, airtight container, away from direct light and excessive heat. It should keep well under these conditions for up to 12 months, although it is best used within 6 months.

Suggested use:

Offer free-choice daily from early spring to late autumn. If adding to the horse's food, give ½ to 1 cupful (1 to 2 oz.) per day for the average-size horse. Transition to *Autumn-Winter Meadow Blend* in late autumn.*

Alternatively, offer some or all of these herbs individually, and allow the horse to choose what and how much to eat each day.

Dried herbs may be rehydrated before feeding, but discard any uneaten portion after 24 hours once water has been added.

Notes:

The herbs in this blend are all safe to feed in larger amounts than those suggested here. The daily amount recommended to feed is intended to be a balance of effectiveness and economy. You can safely feed more than 2 oz./day if you desire.

* I typically recommend feeding *Autumn-Winter Meadow Blend* for only about 3 months each year, straddling the winter solstice (December 21–22 in the northern hemisphere). Transition to *Autumn-Winter* in early November, and then back to *Spring-Summer* in late January. Make the transition gradually, over a week or two.

Autumn-Winter Meadow Blend

This seasonal blend is formulated to provide some of the meadow and woodland plants available to horses during the colder months of the year in temperate climates. It is designed to expand the variety of plant-source nutrients in the horse's diet, using plants or plant parts that are naturally available during the dormant season.

Ingredients:

herbs	proportions	to make 3 lbs	other amount or substitution
couch (dog) grass root	1	4 oz.	
dandelion leaf	1	4 oz.	
dandelion root	1	4 oz.	
elder berries	2	8 oz.	
marshmallow root	2	8 oz.	
red clover leaf & flower	1	4 oz.	
rose hips	2	8 oz.	
sunflower seeds	2	8 oz.	

Instructions:

Measure out all herbs and mix together well. Store the blend in a dry, airtight container, away from direct light and excessive heat. It should keep well under these conditions for up to 12 months, although it is best used within 6 months. (Note: the sunflower seeds make this blend particularly attractive to rodents.)

Suggested use:

Offer free-choice daily from late autumn to early spring. If adding to the horse's food, give 1/3 to 2/3 cupful (1 to 2 oz.) per day for the average-size horse. Transition to *Spring-Summer Meadow Blend* in late winter.*

Alternatively, offer some or all of these herbs individually, and allow the horse to choose what and how much to eat each day.

Dried herbs may be rehydrated before feeding. In fact, adding warm water to this blend makes a very nice winter mash. But be sure to discard any uneaten portion after 24 hours once water has been added.

Notes:

The herbs in this blend are all safe to feed in larger amounts than those suggested here. The daily amount recommended to feed is intended to be a balance of effectiveness and economy. You can safely feed more than 2 oz./day if you desire.

It is usually a good idea to supplement the horse's diet with extra sunflower seeds or some other whole-food source of essential fatty acids during the winter months, when most horses are on a hay-based diet. While sunflower seeds aren't as high in omega-3 fatty acids as some other seeds and nuts, they are economical, easy to find, require no special storage or handling, and are very palatable to horses. Even overweight horses may benefit from up to 1 cupful of sunflower seeds per day.

* I typically recommend feeding *Autumn-Winter Meadow Blend* for only about 3 months each year, straddling the winter solstice (December 21–22 in the northern hemisphere). Transition to *Autumn-Winter* in early November, and then back to *Spring-Summer* in late January. Make the transition gradually, over a week or two.

Competition Blend

This variation of *Spring-Summer Meadow Blend* is specifically formulated for the performance horse. It is designed to support the systems most under stress during training and competition, and to comply with United States Equestrian Federation (USEF) medication rules. This blend contains no herbs prohibited at the time of publication under USEF medication rules.

Ingredients:

herbs	proportions	to make 3 lbs	other amount or substitution
dandelion root	1	4 oz.	
elder berries	2	8 oz.	
fo-ti	1	4 oz.	
hawthorn leaf & flower	1	4 oz.	
marshmallow root	2	8 oz.	
nettle leaf	2	8 oz.	
raspberry leaf	1	4 oz.	
rose hips	2	8 oz.	

Instructions:

Measure out all herbs and mix together well. (Note: dried raspberry leaf tends to clump, so break up any clumps as you mix.) Store the blend in a dry, airtight container, away from direct light and excessive heat. It should keep well under these conditions for up to 12 months, although it is best used within 6 months.

Suggested use:

Offer free-choice daily throughout training and competition. If adding to the horse's food, give ½ to 1 cupful (1 to 2 oz.) per day for maintenance in the average-size horse. Increase during intense training, heavy competition, long-distance travel, and other times of greater than usual stress.

Alternatively, offer some or all of these herbs individually, and allow the horse to choose what and how much to eat each day.

Dried herbs may be rehydrated before feeding, but discard any uneaten portion after 24 hours once water has been added.

Notes:

The herbs in this blend are all safe to feed in larger amounts than those suggested here. The daily amount recommended to feed is intended to be a balance of effectiveness and economy. You can safely feed more than 2 oz./day if you desire.

While *Competition Blend* was not formulated as a medicinal blend and should not be exclusively relied upon as such, it can be a useful aid in preventing illness and facilitating recovery from illness or injury. Amounts of at least 1 cupful (2 oz.) once or twice a day are suggested for the average-size horse in these circumstances. *But check with your veterinarian before using these—or any—herbs in a sick horse.*

Cornucopia

Cornucopia means "horn of plenty." This sumptuous blend is formulated to provide an abundance of nutritive herbs for the chronically depleted or overloaded body. It was inspired by a worn-out old broodmare who was given a new lease on life by the wonderful folks at The Flag Foundation.

Ingredients:

herbs	proportions	to make 3 lbs	other amount or substitution
cleavers	1	4 oz.	
couch (dog) grass root	1	4 oz.	
dandelion leaf	1	4 oz.	
dandelion root	1	4 oz.	
elder berries	1	4 oz.	
hawthorn leaf & flower	1	4 oz.	
marshmallow root	1	4 oz.	
meadowsweet	1	4 oz.	
nettle leaf	1	4 oz.	
raspberry leaf	1	4 oz.	
red clover leaf & flower	1	4 oz.	
rose hips	1	4 oz.	

Instructions:

Measure out all herbs and mix together well. (Note: dried raspberry leaf tends to clump, so break up any clumps as you mix.) Store the blend in a dry, airtight container, away from direct light and excessive heat. It should keep well under these conditions for up to 12 months, although it is best used within 6 months.

Suggested use:

Offer free-choice daily. If adding to the horse's food, start with 1/2 to 1 cupful (1 to 2 oz.) per day for the average-size horse.

Alternatively, offer some or all of these herbs individually, and allow the horse to choose what and how much to eat each day.

Dried herbs may be rehydrated before feeding. In fact, adding warm water to this blend makes a very nice warm mash. But be sure to discard any uneaten portion after 24 hours once water has been added.

Notes:

The herbs in this blend are all safe to feed in larger amounts than those suggested here. The daily amount recommended to feed is intended to be a balance of effectiveness and economy. You can safely feed more than 2 oz./day if you desire.

It is a good idea to supplement the diet with sunflower seeds or some other whole-food source of essential fatty acids if the horse is on a diet of hay or pellets, with little or no fresh grazing or foraging. While sunflower seeds aren't as high in omega-3 fatty acids as some other seeds and nuts, they are economical, easy to find, require no special storage or handling, and are very palatable to horses.

Mobility Blend

This blend is a transitional formulation, somewhere between nutritive and medicinal in design ("food as medicine"). An adaptation of the *Spring-Summer Meadow Blend*, it is formulated to help restore and maintain healthy bones, joints, muscles, and connective tissues, as well as expand the variety of plant-source nutrients in the diet.

Ingredients:

herbs	proportions	to make 3 lbs	other amount or substitution
cleavers	1	4 oz.	
couch (dog) grass root	1	4 oz.	
dandelion root	1	4 oz.	
elder berries	1	4 oz.	
hawthorn leaf & flower	1	4 oz.	
marshmallow root	1	4 oz.	
meadowsweet*	2	8 oz.	
nettle leaf	1	4 oz.	
raspberry leaf	1	4 oz.	
red clover leaf & flower	1	4 oz.	
rose hips	1	4 oz.	

* I mix a combination of meadowsweet herb (leaf and stem) and meadowsweet flower in a ratio of 3:1, so 8 oz. "meadowsweet" = 6 oz. leaf/stem + 2 oz. flower. But you can use one or the other instead.

Instructions:

Measure out all herbs and mix together well. (Note: dried raspberry leaf tends to clump, so break up any clumps as you mix.) Store the blend in a dry, airtight container, away from direct light and excessive heat. It should keep well under these conditions for up to 12 months, although it is best used within 6 months.

Suggested use:

Offer free-choice daily. If adding to the horse's food, begin with ½ cup (1 oz.) twice a day for the average-size horse, then adjust up or down as needed. (Most horses do well on ½ cup per day for maintenance.)

Alternatively, offer some or all of these herbs individually, and allow the horse to choose what and how much to eat each day.

Dried herbs may be rehydrated before feeding. In fact, adding warm water to this blend makes a very nice warm mash. But be sure to discard any uneaten portion after 24 hours once water has been added.

Notes:

The herbs in this blend are all safe to feed in larger amounts than those suggested here. The daily amount recommended to feed is intended to be a balance of effectiveness and economy. You can safely feed more than 2 oz./day if you desire, or if the horse chooses. This blend is a particularly good one to offer free-choice in horses dealing with active inflammation.

USEF competitors, please note: Although none of the herbs in this blend are specifically prohibited under the current USEF medication rules, some of these herbs contain salicylates or other anti-inflammatory substances, so the use of this blend could result in a positive drug test. In horses showing under USEF rules, use it only between shows, allowing a withholding period of at least a week before a show.

Vitality *green*

This green-tinged blend is the original *Vitality* and is formulated to supply horses with supplemental vitamins, trace minerals, enzymes, essential fatty acids, antioxidants, and other cofactors necessary for good health and vitality.

Ingredients (all powdered):

herbs	to make 1 lb	to make 3 lbs	other amount or substitution
azomite	2 oz.	6 oz.	
beet root	1 oz.	3 oz.	
chlorella	6 oz.	18 oz.	
dandelion root	1 oz.	3 oz.	
diatomite	0.5 oz.	1.5 oz.	
dulse or kelp	0.5 oz.	1.5 oz.	
fo-ti	1.5 oz.	4.5 oz.	
garlic	1 oz.	3 oz.	
ginger	0.5 oz.	1.5 oz.	
rose hips	1 oz.	3 oz.	
salt*	0.5 oz.	1.5 oz.	
turmeric	0.5 oz.	1.5 oz.	

* My preference is Himalayan pink salt, Redmond salt, or some other naturally occurring trace-mineral salt.

To make this blend less fly-away, I usually add either lecithin liquid or a combination of lecithin powder and walnut oil, to the desired texture. Vinegar is another option.

Instructions:

Measure out all ingredients and mix together well. Some of these items tend to clump even with proper storage, so sifting the ingredient using a kitchen strainer before adding it to the rest makes blending easier. Alternatively, the finished blend may be sifted after mixing (although that is more laborious). If adding lecithin liquid or a vegetable oil, ensure that the liquid is thoroughly mixed through.

Store the blend in a dry, airtight container, away from direct light and excessive heat. It should keep well at room temperature under these conditions for up to 6 months, although it is best used within 3 months. For longer storage, keep the blend in an airtight container in the fridge or freezer.

Suggested use:

Offer free-choice daily. If adding to the horse's food, give 1–3 tablespoons per day, according to size and need. For chronically depleted bodies, begin with 2–3 tbsp/day for the first few weeks, then reduce to 1–2 tbsp/day for maintenance.

If no lecithin or oil is added to the blend, add a small amount of liquid to the individual portion before feeding, or mix with damp food.

Vitality *red*

This red-tinged blend is a simpler version of *Vitality green,* originally formulated for a very picky eater. (This blend is sweeter and milder in taste.) As with *Vitality green,* it is designed to be an all-natural, primarily whole-food source of essential micronutrients for horses.

Ingredients (all powdered):

herbs	to make 1 lb	to make 3 lbs	other amount or substitution
azomite	3 oz.	9 oz.	
beet root	6 oz.	18 oz.	
chlorella	2 oz.	6 oz.	
dulse	1 oz.	3 oz.	
fo-ti	1.5 oz.	4.5 oz.	
garlic	1 oz.	3 oz.	
rose hips	1 oz.	3 oz.	
salt*	0.5 oz.	1.5 oz.	

* My preference is Himalayan pink salt, Redmond salt, or some other naturally occurring trace-mineral salt.

Instructions:

Measure out all ingredients and mix together well. Some of these items tend to clump even with proper storage, so sifting the ingredient using a kitchen strainer before adding it to the rest makes blending easier. Alternatively, the finished blend may be sifted after mixing (although that is more laborious).

Store the blend in a dry, airtight container, away from direct light and excessive heat. It should keep well at room temperature under these conditions for up to 6 months, although it is best used within 3 months. For longer storage, keep the blend in an airtight container in the fridge or freezer.

Suggested use:

Offer free-choice daily. If adding to the horse's food, give 1–3 tablespoons per day, according to size and need. For chronically depleted bodies, begin with 2–3 tbsp/day for the first few weeks, then reduce to 1–2 tbsp/day for maintenance.

Vitality *canid*

This savory blend is a variation of *Vitality green* that is specifically formulated for dogs. It is designed to be an all-natural, primarily whole-food source of essential micronutrients, with a taste most dogs like. (I like it, too.)

Ingredients (all powdered):

herbs	to make 1 lb	to make 2 lbs	other amount or substitution
azomite	1 oz.	2 oz.	
barley grass	1 oz.	2 oz.	
beet root	2 oz.	4 oz.	
chlorella	6 oz.	12 oz.	
dulse or kelp	0.25 oz.	0.5 oz.	
fo-ti	1 oz.	2 oz.	
garlic	0.5 oz.	1 oz.	
ginger	0.5 oz.	1 oz.	
nutritional yeast	3 oz.	6 oz.	
salt*	0.25 oz.	0.5 oz.	
turmeric	0.5 oz.	1 oz.	

* My preference is Himalayan pink salt, Redmond salt, or some other naturally occurring trace-mineral salt.

If you're feeding a home-made diet and meeting the dog's calcium needs is an issue, then consider adding some diatomite (about 1 oz. per pound of the blend). *But do not rely on this addition—or this blend—to meet the dog's calcium needs.* Supplemental calcium will still be required, such as whole bone, bone meal, or a calcium powder.

Instructions:

Measure out all ingredients and mix together well. Some of these items tend to clump even with proper storage, so sifting the ingredient using a kitchen strainer before adding it to the rest makes blending easier. Alternatively, the finished blend may be sifted after mixing (although that is more laborious).

Lecithin liquid or a combination of lecithin powder and vegetable oil (e.g. walnut oil) may be added to make the blend less fly-away. Add just enough to create the desired texture, mixing the liquid thoroughly with the dry blend.

Store the blend in a dry, airtight container, away from direct light and excessive heat. It should keep well at room temperature under these conditions for up to 6 months, although it is best used within 3 months. For longer storage, keep the blend in an airtight container in the fridge or freezer.

Suggested use:

Add to the dog's food, starting with the following amounts: 1/4 teaspoon (small dogs), 1/2 teaspoon (medium dogs), or 1 teaspoon (large dogs) once a day; adjust up or down as needed.

Notes:

A fish oil or some other tasty animal fat is a more species-appropriate addition than lecithin or a vegetable oil. However, most healthy animal fats/oils don't keep well at room temperature, so if using an animal fat, keep the *Vitality canid* in the fridge.

I'm for simplicity and ease of use, so I've consistently tried to formulate blends that can be kept at room temperature for at least a couple of months without "going off."

❀ ❀ ❀

Herbs as Medicine

The recipes in this chapter were formulated to help restore and maintain health and well-being from particular angles, based on the known effects of the individual herbs and on my knowledge, experience, and perspective as a veterinarian.

There are several different schools of thought when it comes to the medicinal use of herbs. I'm more inclined to the European ("western") schools of traditional and modern herbalism, although I do use some herbs that originated in Chinese or Ayurvedic (Indian) medicine. I'm also really drawn to elements of the Eclectics' approach, which factors in the energetics or essential properties of the plant.

In fact, there are almost as many different ways of using medicinal herbs as there are practitioners of herbal medicine. Personally, I try to follow the KISS principle: "Keep It Simple, Sally!" Each herb used must have a good reason for being there; otherwise, leave it out.

The kitchen-sink approach—of adding anything that *might* be helpful, or including *every* herb that has ever been suggested as being helpful for such-and-such an organ or condition—can confuse a sick body by giving it too many different things to deal with and too many different messages to process. In fact, some of the "big gun" medicinal herbs can be very hard on an ailing system, taking more from the system in processing than they provide in support. These also tend to be the herbs with the narrowest safety margins.

It's also useful to remember that bodies aren't merely collections of separate organs and tissues. They function—and break down—as an integrated whole. Treating only diseased organs instead of diseased bodies is doomed to fail. Although several of the blends in this chapter may seem to be targeted to one organ or body system, all have been formulated to help the whole body return to a healthy state of self-maintenance.

I have been using each of the following blends in my practice for years. However, what was stated at the front of the book bears repeating here:

> The FDA and USDA prohibit claims of nutritional or medicinal benefit for substances they do not regard as "food" or have not approved as "medicine." For this reason, information about the recipes in this chapter is limited to their contents, suggested use, and what I intended when formulating them.
>
> These recipes are not intended to be a substitute for veterinary care. Please partner with a veterinarian to ensure the very best care for your animals.

To avoid repetition, I'll note here that all of the recipes in this chapter use powdered or finely flaked ingredients. I'll also note that my preferred source of salt in these blends is one of the natural trace-mineral salts mined from ancient sea beds, such as Himalayan pink salt or Redmond salt. And again, *organic if possible.*

Cleanse & Restore

This simple blend of herbs, mineral salt, and azomite (a natural clay that contains many different trace elements) is designed to help the body clear itself of metabolic and environmental pollutants, repair any associated cell damage, replenish its trace nutrient stores, and thereby return to good health. It is an adaptation of a protocol used by an MD who works with autistic children and adults with chronic disease.

Ingredients:

herbs	to make 1 lb	to make 2 lbs	other amount or substitution
azomite	2 oz.	4 oz.	
barley grass	1 oz.	2 oz.	
chlorella	6 oz.	12 oz.	
cilantro	3 oz.	6 oz.	
garlic	2 oz.	4 oz.	
salt	1 oz.	2 oz.	
wheat germ*	1 oz.	2 oz.	

* Lecithin can be substituted for the wheat germ if you cannot find any raw, organic wheat germ. However, wheat germ is the better choice, except in animals with wheat intolerance (for whom *Cleanse lite,* the next recipe, was formulated.)

Instructions:

Measure out all ingredients and mix together well. Sift using a kitchen strainer if needed to break up any clumps. Store the blend in a dry, airtight container, away from direct light and excessive heat. It should keep well at room temperature under these conditions for up to 6 months, although it is best used within 3 months. For longer storage, keep the blend in an airtight container in the fridge or freezer.

Suggested use:

Horses (1,000 lbs)—begin with 3 tablespoons (1 oz.) in food once a day; adjust up or down as needed.

Dogs—begin with 1/4 teaspoon (small dogs), 1/2 teaspoon (medium dogs), or 1 teaspoon (large dogs) in food once a day; adjust up or down as needed.

Cats—use *Cleanse lite* instead.

Notes:

Use *Cleanse lite* instead in any animal—cat, dog, or horse—who is sensitive to garlic or wheat. That recipe is on the next page.

The amount of salt used in this blend is designed to encourage the animal to drink extra water, to help with the excretion of waste products and pollutants. So, be sure to provide plenty of fresh, clean (preferably filtered) drinking water when using this blend, and anticipate an increase in urine output.

I typically use *Cleanse & Restore* at the above rates for 2–3 weeks in animals dealing with chronic disease. Depending on the situation, I may extend it another 3 weeks at a lower rate, although most animals do not need it beyond the first 2–3 weeks.

Some of my clients repeat the initial course every 6 months or for 1 week/month. However, while I don't object, I also don't agree with this approach. If the animal's diet and water supply are clean and healthy, then there should be no need for regular use of this primarily medicinal blend. I do not subscribe to the belief that our bodies need a regular "detox." Our food, water, and basic lifestyle should provide ample opportunity for our bodies to cleanse and restore themselves through their innate mechanisms. This blend is for use when we have let those fundamentals slide.

Cleanse *lite*

This blend is *Cleanse & Restore* without the garlic and wheat germ, for animals who are sensitive to either of those ingredients.

Ingredients:

herbs	to make 1 lb	to make 2 lbs	other amount or substitution
azomite	2 oz.	4 oz.	
barley grass	3 oz.	6 oz.	
chlorella	6 oz.	12 oz.	
cilantro	4 oz.	8 oz.	
salt	1 oz.	2 oz.	

Lecithin liquid or powder can be added to make this blend less fly-away. (It is also a useful molecule in its own right, serving both nutritional and medicinal purposes.) Add approximately 1 oz. lecithin per pound, or as much as needed for the desired texture and "mouth feel" (it lends a softness or smoothness when added to strongly flavored herbs).

Instructions:

Measure out all ingredients and mix together well. Sift using a kitchen strainer if needed to break up any clumps. Store the blend in a dry, airtight container, away from direct light and excessive heat. It should keep well at room temperature under these conditions for up to 6 months, although it is best used within 3 months. For longer storage, keep the blend in an airtight container in the fridge or freezer.

Suggested use:

Horses (1,000 lbs)—begin with 3 tablespoons (1 oz.) in food once a day; adjust up or down as needed.

Dogs—begin with 1/4 teaspoon (small dogs), 1/2 teaspoon (medium dogs), or 1 teaspoon (large dogs) in food once a day; adjust up or down as needed.

Cats—begin with a sprinkling and work up to 1/8 teaspoon per day as needed; add to food and mix in well.

Notes:

The amount of salt used in this blend is designed to encourage the animal to drink extra water, to help with the excretion of waste products and pollutants. So, be sure to provide plenty of fresh, clean (preferably filtered) drinking water when using this blend, and anticipate an increase in urine output.

I typically use *Cleanse lite* in the same way as described for *Cleanse & Restore*.

Gluta-Mix

This blend of herbs and glutamine (an amino acid) is formulated to help restore and maintain a healthy stomach and intestinal tract in animals under stress. Glutamine is considered to be a "conditionally essential" amino acid. While it is not one of the essential amino acids (i.e. those that cannot be manufactured "on-board" and so must be provided in the diet), glutamine is thought to become essential during periods of stress, and particularly when there has been damage to the gut lining.

Ingredients:

herbs	to make 1 lb	to make 2 lbs	other amount or substitution
azomite	1.9 oz.	3.8 oz.	
barley grass	1 oz.	2 oz.	
dandelion root	1 oz.	2 oz.	
fo-ti	1 oz.	2 oz.	
L-glutamine	4 oz.	8 oz.	
licorice root	2 oz.	4 oz.	
marshmallow root	4 oz.	8 oz.	
rhodiola	1 oz.	2 oz.	
salt	0.1 oz.	0.2 oz.	

Instructions:

Measure out all ingredients and mix together well. Sift using a kitchen strainer if needed to break up any clumps. Store the blend in a dry, airtight container, away from direct light and excessive heat. It should keep well at room temperature under these conditions for up to 6 months, although it is best used within 3–4 months. For longer storage, keep the blend in an airtight container in the fridge or freezer.

Suggested use:

Horses (1,000 lbs)—begin with 3 tablespoons (1 oz.) in food twice a day; adjust up or down as needed for maintenance. (Most horses do well on 1 tbsp once or twice a day for maintenance.)

Dogs—begin with 1/4 teaspoon (small dogs), 1/2 teaspoon (medium dogs), or 1 teaspoon (large dogs) in food once or twice a day as needed; adjust up or down as needed for maintenance.

Cats—begin with a sprinkling and work up to 1/8 teaspoon per day as needed; add to food and mix in well.

Notes:

This blend has a mild nutty, slightly sweet flavor. Horses love it, and dogs and cats eat it well, too.

Because *Gluta-Mix* contains licorice root, which can cause problems with adrenal gland function at high doses or with prolonged use, I typically recommend phasing it out as soon as the animal can do without it. My guiding philosophy with all things medicinal is this: *use only what is needed, for only as long as needed.* Be always on the lookout for the point at which this—or any—intervention can safely be removed.

USEF/FEI* competitors, please note: none of the herbs in this blend are specifically prohibited under the current USEF medication rules. However, use of any such blend may contravene the *spirit* of the rules for FEI events. For this reason, I advise suspending the use of this blend in the week before an FEI event.

(* Fédération Equestre Internationale, or International Equestrian Federation)

Green Magic

This green-colored blend of herbs and a broad-spectrum probiotic is designed to help restore and maintain a healthy liver and intestinal tract. (I was in one of those lovely silly moods the day I named it.) In terms of its "energetic" effect, it is gently cooling.

Ingredients:

herbs	to make 1 lb	to make 2 lbs	other amount or substitution
azomite	3 oz.	6 oz.	
barley grass	2.5 oz.	5 oz.	
chlorella	6 oz.	12 oz.	
dandelion root	1 oz.	2 oz.	
elder berries	2 oz.	4 oz.	
salt	0.5 oz.	1 oz.	
probiotic blend*	1 oz.	2 oz.	

* I use Primal Defense (made by Garden of Life), as it is a broad-spectrum probiotic blend consisting of about a dozen different microbial species, most of which are considered homeostatic soil organisms (i.e. the types of microbes we'd naturally be getting on or in our food were we to be eating our food fresh and in its natural state).

Instructions:

Measure out all ingredients and mix together well. Sift using a kitchen strainer if needed to break up any clumps. Store the blend in a dry, airtight container, away from direct light and excessive heat. It should keep well at room temperature under these conditions for up to 6 months, although it is best used within 3 months. For longer storage, keep the blend in an airtight container in the fridge or freezer.

Suggested use:

Horses (1,000 lbs)—begin with 1 tablespoon in food once or twice a day; adjust up or down as needed. Provide plenty of good-quality forages as well.

Dogs—begin with 1/4 teaspoon (small dogs), 1/2 teaspoon (medium dogs), or 1 teaspoon (large dogs) in food once a day; adjust up or down as needed.

Cats—begin with a sprinkling and work up to 1/8 teaspoon per day as needed; add to food and mix in well.

Notes:

I use *Green Magic* or the *lite* version (next page) to support a return to healthy digestive function, along with whatever diet and lifestyle changes are needed. This blend is not enough on its own if the basic diet and lifestyle (e.g. daily turnout for horses, daily exercise for all species) are not appropriate for the animal. And this blend is no substitute for full-strength probiotic therapy when such is needed.

Green Magic *lite*

This blend is basically *Green Magic* without the probiotic. It is designed to support healthy liver and intestinal function in animals who would not benefit from the addition of probiotics. As with *Green Magic* regular, this blend is gently "cooling."

Ingredients:

herbs	to make 1 lb	to make 2 lbs	other amount or substitution
azomite	3 oz.	6 oz.	
barley grass	2 oz.	4 oz.	
chlorella	6 oz.	12 oz.	
dandelion root	1 oz.	2 oz.	
elder berries	1 oz.	2 oz.	
L-glutamine	2 oz.	4 oz.	
licorice root	0.5 oz.	1 oz.	
salt	0.5 oz.	1 oz.	

Instructions:

Measure out all ingredients and mix together well. Sift using a kitchen strainer if needed to break up any clumps. Store the blend in a dry, airtight container, away from direct light and excessive heat. It should keep well at room temperature under these conditions for up to 6 months, although it is best used within 3–4 months. For longer storage, keep the blend in an airtight container in the fridge or freezer.

Suggested use:

Horses (1,000 lbs)—begin with 1 tablespoon in food once or twice a day; adjust up or down as needed. Provide plenty of good-quality forages as well.

Dogs—begin with 1/4 teaspoon (small dogs), 1/2 teaspoon (medium dogs), or 1 teaspoon (large dogs) in food once a day; adjust up or down as needed.

Cats—begin with a sprinkling and work up to 1/8 teaspoon per day as needed; add to food and mix in well.

Notes:

I use *Green Magic lite* to support a return to healthy digestive function, along with whatever diet and lifestyle changes are needed. As with *Green Magic* regular, this blend is not enough on its own if the basic diet and lifestyle are not appropriate for the animal. And sometimes *Cleanse & Restore* is the better choice.

Spicy Magic

This spicy blend of antioxidant-rich herbs is designed to invigorate a sluggish system; to help restore and maintain healthy circulation, metabolism, and digestion; and to counter oxidative stress. (As with *Green Magic,* I was in one of those delightfully silly moods the day I named it.) In terms of its energetics, this blend is gently "warming."

Ingredients:

herbs	to make 1 lb	to make 3 lbs	other amount or substitution
fo-ti	1.4 oz.	4 oz.	
ginger	1.3 oz.	4 oz.	
hawthorn berry	4 oz.	12 oz.	
lecithin	1.4 oz.	4 oz.	
licorice root	0.3 oz.	1 oz.	
mace	0.3 oz.	1 oz.	
marshmallow root	2 oz.	6 oz.	
rose hips	2.7 oz.	8 oz.	
salt	1.3 oz.	4 oz.	
turmeric	1.3 oz.	4 oz.	

Instructions:

Measure out all ingredients and mix together well. Sift using a kitchen strainer if needed to break up any clumps. Store the blend in a dry, airtight container, away from direct light and excessive heat. It should keep well at room temperature under these conditions for up to 6 months, although it is best used within 3–4 months. For longer storage, keep the blend in an airtight container in the fridge or freezer.

Suggested use:

Horses (1,000 lbs)—begin with 1 tablespoon in food twice a day; adjust up or down as needed. (Most horses do well with 1 tbsp once a day for maintenance.)

Notes:

I use this blend quite a lot in senior horses, particularly during the colder months, and in athletes. As it is a warming blend, I advise using it very sparingly during the summer, especially in working horses. I also use this blend or a simpler version of it in grey horses with masses that are presumed to be melanomas.

Vitex Plus

This blend of chasteberry *(Vitex agnus-castus)* and other herbs is designed to help with central regulation of the endocrine (hormonal) system in older horses.

Ingredients:

herbs	to make 1 lb	to make 2 lbs	other amount or substitution
barley grass	2 oz.	4 oz.	
chasteberry (Vitex)	2.5 oz.	5 oz.	
dandelion root	1 oz.	2 oz.	
dulse	0.25 oz.	0.5 oz.	
ginger	0.25 oz.	0.5 oz.	
hawthorn berry	1 oz.	2 oz.	
lecithin	1 oz.	2 oz.	
licorice root	1 oz.	2 oz.	
maca	1 oz.	2 oz.	
mucuna	4 oz.	8 oz.	
rose hips	1 oz.	2 oz.	
salt	1 oz.	2 oz.	

Instructions:

Measure out all ingredients and mix together well. Sift using a kitchen strainer if needed to break up any clumps. Store the blend in a dry, airtight container, away from direct light and excessive heat. It should keep well at room temperature under these conditions for up to 6 months, although it is best used within 3–4 months. For longer storage, keep the blend in an airtight container in the fridge or freezer.

Suggested use:

Horses (1,000 lbs)—begin with 1 tablespoon in food twice a day; adjust up or down as needed.*

Notes:

The "powerhouse" herbs in this blend have a very strong flavor (at least, to my taste buds). While some of the other ingredients are included primarily for taste, it may be necessary when feeding this blend to add a small amount of sweetener, such as diluted molasses or honey, to " help the medicine go down."

* When using this blend—or indeed any herbs—with pergolide or other conventional medications for endocrine system regulation, please consult a veterinarian who is experienced with using herbs in horses.

While this blend is a good foundation, I seldom use it exactly as written anymore. Instead, I prefer to custom-blend for each horse according to his/her individual needs, which often change with the season and with alterations in health status (including improvement).

❀ ❀ ❀ ❀

Glossary

Below are the botanical names for the herbs used in these recipes, along with some notes on which part(s) of the plant to use. Different parts of a plant sometimes have different nutritional or medicinal properties, so use the plant part given in the recipe, unless you are familiar enough with herbs to make a suitable substitution.

Also listed are some notes on the other ingredients used in these recipes. For simplicity, all of the ingredients used in this book are listed in alphabetical order.

Azomite—a naturally occurring powdered rock that contains over 70 different minerals and trace elements. Its name is an acronym for "A to Z of minerals and trace elements." It is mined in Utah.

Barley grass—*Hordeum vulgare* leaf and stem, powdered.

Beet root—*Beta vulgaris* root, powdered. (Note that the herb used in these recipes is not beet juice or beet pulp; it's the whole beet root, dried and powdered.)

Chasteberry—*Vitex agnus-castus* berries, powdered.

Chlorella—*Chlorella pyrenoidosa* or *C. vulgaris*. Chlorella organisms are dark-green freshwater microalgae that are rich in micronutrients. Unless a variety with a thin cell wall is used, buy chlorella that has had its thick cell wall broken in some way (e.g. high pressure or sound waves); otherwise it is resistant to digestion. Horses can probably manage, but dogs and cats probably cannot.

* Note: most chlorella sold in the US comes from Asia. Since the 2011 earthquake and nuclear power plant leak in Japan, be sure to confirm the source and safety of any chlorella you buy from Asia.

Cilantro—*Coriandrum sativum* leaf and stem, powdered.

Cleavers—*Galium aparine* leaf and stem, whole or cut (i.e. not powdered).

Couch/dog grass root—*Agropyron repens* root, whole or cut. Called couch grass or dog grass.

Dandelion—*Taraxacum officinale*. The recipe will specify whether to use the leaf, the root, or both. The Leafy Blends in Chapter 2 use cut leaf, cut root, or both. All of the other blends containing dandelion use the powdered root.

Diatomite—a naturally occurring powdered sedimentary rock that is composed of the fossilized remains of tiny, hard-shelled algae called diatoms ("di-atoms"). Also known as "diatomaceous earth." Diatomite is rich in silica and other minerals. Be sure to buy only <u>food-grade</u> diatomite, as the industrial grade is abrasive and therefore unsafe for consumption.

Dulse—*Rhodymenia palmetta* or *Palmaria palmata,* powdered. Dulse is a reddish purple marine algae or sea vegetable.

Elder berries—*Sambucus nigra* berries, whole or powdered, depending on the recipe. The Leafy Blends in Chapter 2 use whole berries; the two other blends that contain elder berries use powdered berries.

Fo-ti—*Polygonum multiflorum* root. Also known by its traditional Chinese medicine name, "he/ho shou wu." Use the cured form of the root, powdered in most recipes and finely chopped in *Competition Blend*.

Garlic—*Allium sativum* root/bulb, powdered.

Ginger—*Zingiber officinale* root, powdered.

Glutamine—an amino acid. Also labeled L-glutamine. It is supplied as a white powder. Choose a product that is 100% L-glutamine; no filler or other additives.

Kelp—*Ascophyllum nodosum,* powdered. Kelp is one of several green marine algae or sea vegetables.

Hawthorn—*Crataegus sp.* Use the whole/cut leaf & flower or the powdered berries, depending on the recipe. The Leafy Blends in Chapter 2 use whole/cut leaf & flower; all of the other blends containing hawthorn use the berries, powdered.

Lecithin—a naturally occurring phospholipid, used as an emulsifier and protectant. Most vegetarian sources are derived from soy beans. Lecithin from sunflower seeds is becoming more widely available. Be sure to buy lecithin that is certified not from GMO (genetically modified organisms) or GE (genetically engineered) crops.

Licorice—*Glycyrrhiza glabra* root, powdered.

Maca—*Lepidum meyenii* root, powdered.

Mace—*Myristica fragrans,* powdered. Mace is the fruity tissue surrounding the seed we know as nutmeg. Nutmeg is a suitable substitute if mace cannot be found.

Marshmallow root—*Althea officinalis* root. Use cut or powdered, depending on the recipe. The Leafy Blends in Chapter 2 use the cut root; all other recipes containing marshmallow root use the powdered root.

Meadowsweet—*Filipendula ulmaria.* Use the leaf or "herb" (leaf and stem), with or without a little of the flower, which typically is sold as a separate herb. Meadowsweet flower usually is quite a bit more expensive than the leaf/stem, but it is well worth buying a little of the flower as well. (See *Mobility Blend* in Chapter 2.)

Mucuna—*Mucuna pruriens* bean (cotyledon), powdered.

Nettle leaf—*Urtica dioica* or other common *Urtica* species. All of the recipes containing nettles use the leaf or herb (leaf and stem), not the root or seed. Some suppliers list nettle leaf as "leaf"; others list it as nettle "herb" or simply "nettles."

Nutritional yeast—*Saccharomyces cerevisiae,* powdered or finely flaked.

Raspberry leaf—*Rubus idaeus* leaf, whole or cut.

Red Clover—*Trifolium pratense.* Red clover is most often supplied as "herb," meaning mostly leaf and stem, perhaps with a little flower mixed in. Red clover flower or "blossom" as a separate item is wonderful but expensive, so buy red clover herb/leaf, and perhaps splurge on a few ounces of red clover blossoms from time to time if you don't have clovers growing where your horse lives.

Rhodiola—*Rhodiola rosea* root, powdered.

Rose hips—*Rosa canina* fruit (hips), either whole/cut or powdered, depending on the recipe. The Leafy Blends in Chapter 2 use whole or cut rosehips; all other recipes containing rose hips use the powdered form.

Salt—salt is used in these recipes for flavor, to encourage drinking, and as a supplemental source of trace minerals. For the latter reason, I recommend using a natural trace-mineral salt, such as Himalayan pink salt or Redmond salt, mined from ancient sea beds rather than salt extracted from our now-polluted oceans.

Sunflower seeds—*Helianthus annuus* seeds, either hulled or still in their shells. The shells are so soft, it makes little difference to most horses.

Turmeric—*Curcuma longa* root, powdered.

Vitex—*Vitex agnus-castus* berries, powdered. Also called chasteberry or chaste tree.

Wheat germ—*Triticum aestivum* germ. Try to find raw, organic wheat germ, or at least raw wheat germ from certified non-GMO or non-GE wheat. After opening the bag, store the remainder in the fridge or freezer in an airtight container.

❋ ❋ ❋ ❋ ❋

Sources

Grow your own

If possible, grow as many of your own herbs as you can, both in garden beds and in your pastures, around the barn, along fence lines, in ditches, and in other "wasted" spaces where your horses live. Not only will you be providing your horses with a variety of fresh herbs in season, but you'll be adding to the fertility of your soils, which is a great investment in your horses' health.

There are many excellent books and on-line sources of information about growing, harvesting, and drying herbs. Do some research before planting so that you don't accidentally introduce potentially invasive species to your area. County extension agents usually are a great asset in helping you decide what to plant, and what not to plant, on your farm.

Wildcrafting

Wildcrafting is another way of providing your horse with fresh herbs. Wildcrafting simply means to collect plant material from "the wild." The simplest way is to allow your horse to browse among the "weeds" along the edges of fields, lanes, and other untended areas, or let him snap up whatever appeals when you're out on a trail ride. I recommend this approach for horses recovering from various ailments, including laminitis. Horses will often self-medicate when given an opportunity. Just be sure to avoid areas that have been sprayed with pesticides or herbicides. And, of course, avoid plants that are toxic to horses.

If you live in an area with an abundance of wild plants, then plan a herb-picking day, feeding some of the collected herbs fresh that day and drying the rest for later.

When wildcrafting, be respectful of the plants you harvest and the ecosystem of which they are a part. Before heading out, do some research on how to responsibly harvest wild plants, including correct plant identification, when to harvest, what to harvest, how much to take, and what to leave.

Here are two excellent resources:

❀ *From Earth to Herbalist: an earth-conscious guide to medicinal plants*, by Gregory Tilford

❀ United Plant Savers web site: unitedplantsavers.org

Buying dried herbs in bulk

Although I do grow some herbs myself and carefully wildcraft others, for the recipes in this book I mostly use dried herbs that I buy in bulk. Here are some reputable bulk herb suppliers in the US:

❀ Frontier Natural Products Co-op: frontiercoop.com

❀ Mountain Rose Herbs: mountainroseherbs.com

❀ Pacific Botanicals: pacificbotanicals.com

❀ Starwest Botanicals: starwest-botanicals.com

There are other suppliers of good-quality organic herbs in bulk; these are just the ones I've come to rely on for their herb quality. As much as you can, support the growers and suppliers in your area. And buy organic whenever possible.

Other ingredients

Several of the powdered blends use ingredients other than herbs. Here are the sources I use for those other ingredients:

azomite—Azomite Mineral Products (azomite.com); check on their web site or at local organic garden supply and feed stores to find a supplier near you.

diatomite (diatomaceous earth)—can usually be found at organic garden supply stores and some feed stores, and at various sites on-line. Be sure to buy *food grade,* not industrial grade.

glutamine (L-glutamine)—can be found in bulk (1+ lb tubs) at most health food stores and stores that cater to body builders. Make sure the product you buy is pure L-glutamine; no fillers or additives.

lecithin—Mountain Rose Herbs; can also be found at many natural grocery stores, and at various other on-line sites.

nutritional yeast—can usually be found at natural grocery or health food stores, and at various sites on-line.

Primal Defense—made by Garden of Life; can be found at most health food stores, and at various on-line sites. For ease of use in animals, buy the powder, not the caplets or capsules.

trace-mineral salt—Mountain Rose Herbs; can also be found at many natural grocery stores, and at various other on-line sites.

Other supplies

To save you some time and trouble, here are some supplies and other items that make preparing these herbal blends easier:

❦ a dry, well-ventilated work area where you can make a mess—preferably somewhere with no draft or wind while you're working

❦ dust mask—available at home improvement stores and some drug stores; also use protective eyewear if your eyes are particularly sensitive

❦ old clothes—you're going to get quite messy

❦ 5 gallon bucket or other large container for mixing—if you sift the individual dry ingredients as you go, then one bucket is sufficient; if you're sifting the finished blend, then you'll need a second container

❦ digital scale—use one that measures between 0.1 oz. and 5 lbs; a small postal scale is adequate and not very expensive; available at most office supply stores

❀ large bowl—for weighing the individual herbs on the scale

❀ measuring cups or scoops—these are particularly useful with the powdered herbs

❀ sieve or kitchen strainer—for sifting any dried ingredients that have clumped

❀ storage containers, various sizes—while the individual herbs and the blends can be stored in plastic bags, even better are airtight glass, ceramic, enamel-coated, or stainless steel containers that prevent light (especially UV light) from reaching the herbs; if clear containers are used, store the herbs in a dark cabinet or box, where rodents, cockroaches, etc. can't get to them

❀ labels—I wish I had a dollar for every time I didn't bother to label a bag of herbs, thinking that surely I'd remember what it contained... label everything! Write what the bag contains and the date on which the item was bagged.

Acknowledgements

My deepest appreciation goes to my patients, who have been my greatest teachers and very often my unwitting guinea pigs. My gratitude also goes to the clients who have trusted me enough to let me explore and learn by experience in this beautiful garden of life.

Thanks also to my many human mentors, some of whom I'll never get to meet. They include Dr. Nicholas Larkins, Hilary Page Self, Juliette de Baïracli Levy, and Anny Schneider. No doubt I'm making some outrageous omissions. Blame my lapse in memory rather than my ingratitude.

CPSIA information can be obtained
at www.ICGtesting.com
Printed in the USA
LVOW09s2352130917
548679LV00001B/3/P